YOUNG ENGINEERS

Building Bridges

by Tammy Enz

raintree
a Capstone company — publishers for children

D0229191

Raintree is an imprint of Capstone Global Library Limited, a company incorporated in England and Wales having its registered office at 264 Banbury Road, Oxford OX2 7DY – Registered company number: 6695582

www.raintree.co.uk
myorders@raintree.co.uk

Edited by Adrian Vigliano
Designed by Philippa Jenkins
Picture research by Svetlana Zhurkin
Production by Katy LaVigne
Originated by Capstone Global Library Ltd
Printed and bound in China

ISBN 978 1 4747 3703 6
21 20 19 18 17
10 9 8 7 6 5 4 3 2 1

British Library Cataloguing in Publication Data
A full catalogue record for this book is available from the British Library.

Acknowledgements
We would like to thank the following for permission to reproduce photographs:
Capstone Studio: Karon Dubke, cover, 8, 9, 10, 11, 14, 15, 18, 19, 22, 23, 26, 27; Shutterstock: Checubus, 21, Galina 2703, 13, Leonard Zhukovsky, 25, Mariusz S. Jurgielewicz, 7, mozakim, 29, Roger Zhang, 17, Travel Stock, 5

We would like to thank Harold Pratt for his help in the preparation of this book.

Every effort has been made to contact copyright holders of material reproduced in this book. Any omissions will be rectified in subsequent printings if notice is given to the publisher.

All the internet addresses (URLs) given in this book were valid at the time of going to press. However, due to the dynamic nature of the internet, some addresses may have changed, or sites may have changed or ceased to exist since publication. While the author and publisher regret any inconvenience this may cause readers, no responsibility for any such changes can be accepted by either the author or the publisher.

Contents

Some words are shown in bold, **like this.** You can find out what they mean by looking in the glossary.

What is a bridge?

Many of us use bridges every day. We use them to cross rivers, valleys, train tracks or roads. Bridges can be huge structures spanning miles or simple beams crossing a stream. But all have three basic parts: a **deck, supports** and **structure.**

support

structure

deck

This is the Golden Gate Bridge in San Francisco, USA. It is a suspension bridge.

5

Types of bridges

Many factors affect the type of bridge used. Engineers consider the **span** length, cost and looks. Two types of bridges you often see are **truss bridges** and **suspension bridges.** You might also see beam bridges or **arch bridges.** What other kinds of bridges can you find?

The arch bridge is one of the most common bridge designs in the world.

Experiment with trusses

Truss bridges are made from small pieces of metal connected together to form triangles. Test the strength of triangles in this experiment.

You will need:
- Four sheets of sugar paper
- Books for stacking
- Tape

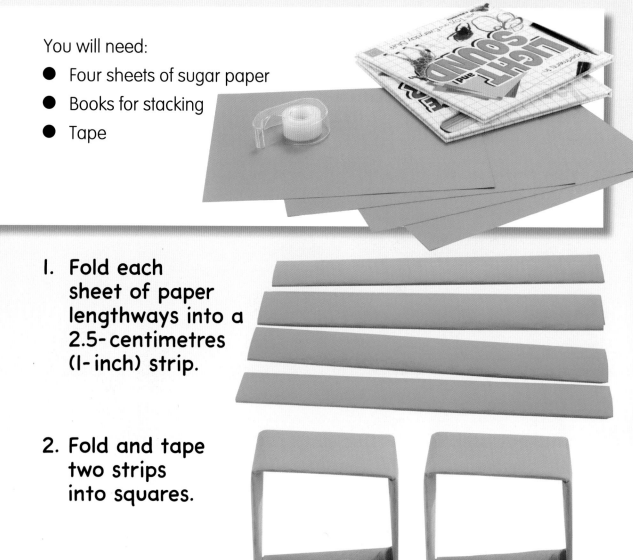

1. Fold each sheet of paper lengthways into a 2.5-centimetres (1-inch) strip.

2. Fold and tape two strips into squares.

3. Set the two squares side by side. Stack books on top until the squares flatten. How many books can the squares hold?

4. Fold and tape the other strips into triangles.

5. Stack books on top of the triangles. Are the triangles stronger?

Build a suspension bridge

Suspension bridges can span farther than simple beam bridges. See how cables make this possible.

You will need:

- Piece of thin cardboard 30 cm (12 in) x 10 cm (4 in)
- Two book stacks
- 4–8 small toy cars
- Four bendable drinking straws with 1 cm (½ inch) slits in their long ends
- Two 60 cm- (24 in-) long strings

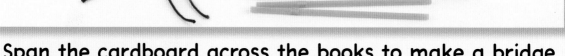

1. Span the cardboard across the books to make a bridge.
2. Place some toy cars on it. How many can it hold?

3. Stick the bendy part of each straw under the stacked books at the bridge ends. (Tape them in place if needed.)
4. Tape each string's centre to one side of the bridge's middle.
5. Thread the strings into the slits in the straws and past the book stacks. Pull the strings tight. Tape their ends down.
6. Now how many cars can the bridge hold?

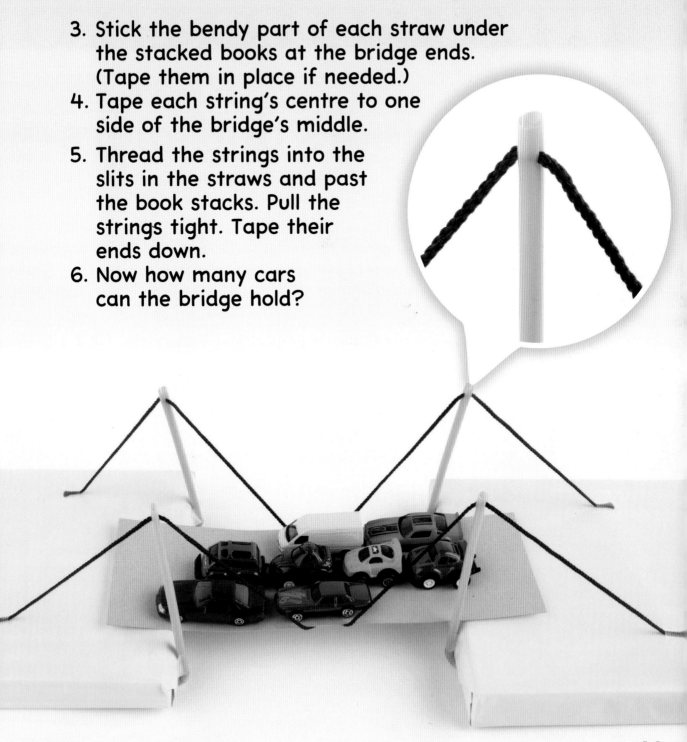

Abutments and piers

It's easy to see many parts of a bridge. But just as important are the parts you don't see. To carry their massive loads, bridges need to be anchored firmly to the ground. Their ends sit on concrete **abutments**. These abutments are buried deep in the ground. They anchor a bridge's weight to rock layers below.

Abutments are designed to support the full weight of a bridge and the things it carries.

abutments

Experiments with abutments

Try this experiment to see how abutments are key to strong bridges.

You will need:

- Two pillows
- A piece of sturdy cardboard about 30 cm (12 in) x 10 cm (4 in)
- 4–6 small toy cars
- Two book stacks

1. Place the pillows about 25 cm (10 in) apart.
   Create a span between them with the cardboard.
2. Place several cars on the cardboard bridge.
   How sturdy is the bridge?

3. Now place the book stacks 25 cm (10 in) apart.
   Create a span between them with the cardboard.
4. Place several cars on the bridge. Do sturdier
   supports make the bridge sturdier?

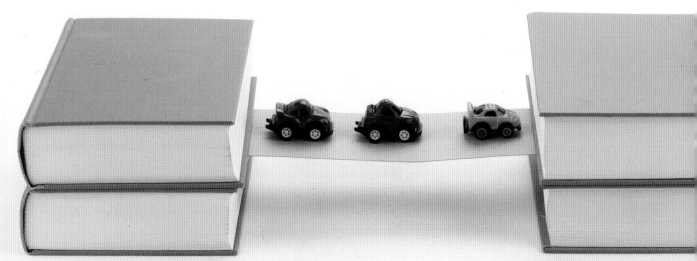

Some bridges can span from one side of a river to the other. But often bridges need middle supports. These **piers** go through the water and mud to rest on rock layers far below the riverbed. Piers are tricky to build. Sometimes workers build a steel box in the river. They pump out all the water and go inside to build piers. Other times piers are drilled from barges.

piers

Piers work with abutments to balance the weight of a long bridge.

17

Make a drilled pier

A drilled pier is made by drilling a steel tube into a riverbed. It is then filled with concrete to make it strong. Test it out with this experiment.

You will need:

- A large container
- Sand
- Cardboard kitchen roll core
- Jug
- Books

1. Fill the container with about 8 cm (3 in) of sand to make a riverbed.
2. Twist the kitchen roll core to drill into the sand to the bottom of the container.
3. Fill the pitcher with sand, and pour it into the tube to fill it.
4. How strong is your pier? Do you need to hold the tube upright? Test it out by stacking books on top.

Expansion joints

Construction materials **expand** when they heat up and **shrink** when cooled down. Bridges are built with expansion joints near their supports. These toothed joints let the bridge expand in summer so its deck doesn't buckle. Expansion joints also let the bridge shrink in winter without making a gap in the road.

Bridge expansion joints allow building materials to expand and contract without cracking.

21

Experiment with expansion and shrinking

Expansion and shrinking caused by heating and cooling are easy to see with this experiment.

You will need:

- Empty glass jar with metal screw-on lid
- Freezer
- Shallow dish filled up to 2.5 cm (1 in) with very hot tap water

1. Screw the lid very tightly on to the jar. Place it in the freezer for 30 minutes.
2. Take it out, and try to unscrew the lid. Can you do it? The cold metal has shrunk, making the lid fit tighter on the jar.

3. Quickly turn the jar upside down in the dish of hot water. Leave it there for 5 minutes. Now try to remove the lid. What happens? Has the warm metal expanded enough to make it come off easily?

Connections

Many small pieces are connected together to make a bridge. **Welds, bolts** and **rivets** are some of the most common connections used. Welds are joints made by heating two metal pieces and melting them together. **Nuts** are threaded on to bolts to help them hold bridge pieces together. A rivet is a pin with a head. It is like a bolt except one end is squashed to hold it in place.

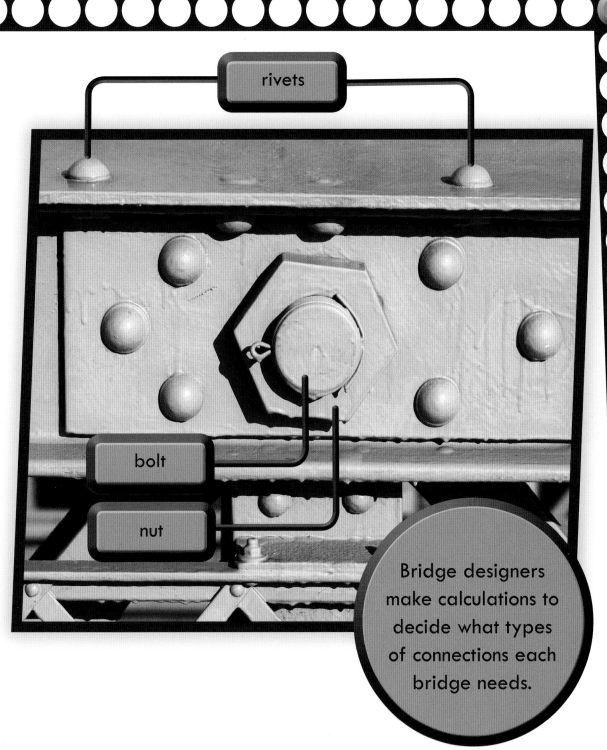

rivets

bolt

nut

Bridge designers make calculations to decide what types of connections each bridge needs.

Make some rivets

See how rivets work to connect two cardboard pieces in this project.

You will need:

- Two thin pieces of cardboard
- Hole punch
- Clay or play-dough

1. Stack the cardboard pieces, and punch three holes through both.
2. Unstack the pieces, and flip one over. Line up the holes.
3. Roll some clay into a very thin string.

4. Cut the clay into three 2.5-cm (1-inch) sections.

5. Thread each section through one of the holes. Squash its ends to make a rivet.
6. Let the clay dry overnight. Test the rivets by gently pulling on the cardboard pieces.

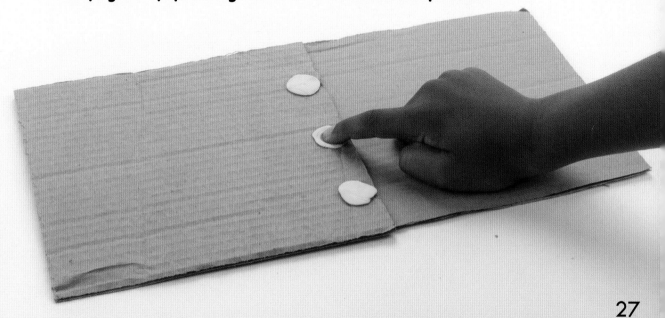

Bridges help us safely cross rivers and roads. Their shapes and structures are carefully designed. They must span great distances and carry heavy loads. But they are more than that. Their unique designs add beauty to cities and country roads.

There are amazing bridges to see all around the world.

Glossary

abutment anchor at a bridge's end

arch bridge curve-shaped bridge

bolt metal pin

deck part of a bridge you walk or drive on

expand get larger

nut part that screws on to a bolt to keep the bolt tight

pier upright support under a bridge

rivet metal pin with flattened ends

shrink get smaller

span length of a bridge

structure part of a bridge that holds up its deck

support part of a bridge that carries its weight to the ground

suspension bridge bridge supported by cables

truss bridge bridge made with triangular shapes

weld connection made by melting metal pieces together

Find out more

Books

Buildings, Bridges and Tunnels (It'll Never Work), Jon
  Richards (Franklin Watts, 2016)

Man-Made Wonders (Worldwide Wonders), (Wayland,
  2016)

The World's Most Amazing Bridges (Landmark Top Tens),
  Michael Hurley (Raintree, 2012)

Websites

www.bbc.co.uk/education/clips/zjvfb9q
Watch this video to find out about the different materials
used to make bridges.

**www.bbc.co.uk/schools/primaryhistory/
famouspeople/isambard_kingdom_brunel**
Learn about Isambard Kingdom Brunel, a famous
engineer who built bridges, tunnels, railways, docks and
ships.

Index